REMARKS *to a*
DANISH PRINCE

Selected Poems by

Christopher Hottel

Designed and produced by:
Indie Author Books
12 High Street, Thomaston, Maine
www.indieauthorbooks.com

Printed in the United States of America

REMARKS *to a* DANISH PRINCE

TABLE OF CONTENTS

Rock Songs 1

The Lanterns *in the* Dark Forest 41

tomb (loom) 79

Eleven Lyrics, One Prelude 105

Nine Poems *in a* Boston Winter 119

Elegy 131

The Persephone Sonnets 135

Remarks *to a* Danish Prince 155

Translations 169
   Greek Choral Fragments:
     Aeschylus, Sophocles, Pindar 169
   The Seafarer: From the Anglo-Saxon 199
     Translation Notes 205

Index of First Lines 213

Rock Songs

Vos lene consilium et datis et dato Gaudetis, almae.

—Horace, Ode 3.4

Who
will ever understand you,
silent
like the poets
when you speak?
And the clocks
you hate,
their silly faces
try to pin you down.
There is a cry in the night,
the shades
are down,
and I whisper,
Where are you? Where are you?
in the dawn.

I have taken
all the rocks
you love,
(I found them
In the quarry
where you left them)
and built a castle.
Now the moon
is shining
over the moat,
on the black water.
Come,
I think it is calling
for us.

What art is this?
The bones of our mother,
the rocks of the earth.
Falling,
falling,
the invisible shelters
of our skin,
you, I.
You turn in your sleep.
The planets
hang
like lanterns
in the night.

— 4 —

In the grotto against the mountain
a spring falls
over the rocks
(they cry their hearts out)
Yes, you have been
there too,
and I hear that
we both have been invited
by the rocks
to join their silent company.

Under the hill
I can hear
the hearts of the rocks
beating.
And the sea
is in my ear too.
O, don't wait, don't wait.
The river
washes you on,
and the blood
flows all black
from my veins.

— 6 —

The shadow
of the rose-bush
waves on the sidewalk,
and I have thought,
no, I will not
go to you tonight.
How blue the sky is!
O my wishing-well,
I have no pennies
to throw.

A cotton dress, up and over,
how simple!
I chisel in the stone
for years,
always refining, refining.
Where are you,
O my dark flesh
caught in the stone?

A drawing
of rainbow fish
and the rocks like hollow spheres
of space
on the shore.
(The dinner
is being prepared
in the ocean tonight)
Your tracing-paper,
leaves of
an artist's tome of life,
butterflies' wings.

Where? How? When?
No.
You put out
my words like candles,
and your
nightgown flies
in the breeze.
Midnight,
a moth is beating himself
against the window.
And death?
My tongue
trapped
between my teeth.

The needle
of the compass twirls
in its magnetic field,
(the ship
which plows
the dolphin-sea,
O sleepy star,
points to you)
What do you say?
Nothing.
I will weave a blanket
of poems
to keep you warm.

While I sit
in my shade
under a pine tree
(through
the cushion of needles
patches of clover
grow)
I go
looking for you
(over
the brinks of waterfalls)
everywhere.

In the room
at the end of the corridor,
the voices
whisper
above the knocking
in the radiator
pipes.
I laugh,
a sky, a parachute.
You stand
so nonchalantly
holding
your pocket mirror
up to my face.

I had to erase
my life
across this page
before I could write
these words.
And the colors
shine so brilliantly
out in the field,
wild strawberry bushes,
the grain,
the country road
with its little spires
of dust,
even the wire-fence,
its wooden posts
eaten away,
a slow singing of crickets,
summer,
I wish to god that I had not.

— 14 —

The church music,
an organ.
You are painting,
coloring
all these solid blocks
of space:
yes,
a mountain,
a field.
The field drips its yellow paint
in little gullies
into the sea.
Is it an accident,
one thing begins
before another ends?

— 15 —

In the Fun House

Rows of vertical mirrors.
Which one
is really you?
The bells ring
under the sea,
and I may have to break
every glass
(the reflections
are born like twins)
to straighten you out
of these
rows and rows of yourselves.

The flowers
drove their stems
like nails
into his little grave.
You only cried.
And the snow
kept whispering of another world
lost in the white ravines.
And when
you grew faint,
I put my arms around you
and held you
so you wouldn't fall,
walking
the long cemetery road
where
only these flowers
break the surface
of the white fields
of snow.

— 17 —

You turn over
into my hands,
and the leaves in the folds
of the sheets
begin to stir.
I dissect my feeling of love,
at first so vague
in your presence,
into
the thousand curiosities
of my hands
moving across
your flesh.
While into the fallow fields
the rain falls
like broken glass.

There are herds of horses
outside your window.
You are a child again.
Around and around
the wheel of time
spins,
the horses
fall
into the purple dusk.
The pasture is parallel
to your breath,
and the window
is no window at all.

O violet flower,
(sudden arms,
petals)
now my voice begins
to elbow
its way into your world,
happy
because you are
everything you want to be.
Not-
withstanding,
I build
a little ship of letters
for you
to sail the seas with.

In the woods,
only a few insects buzzing,
the hollow echoes
of a bird's call
decaying
through the trees.
A spider
bobs on its thread,
hung from a high branch.
So lazy are
these days
in the summer sun,
so lazy,
so lazy.

Divine
is the archer's body
as he pulls his bow.
What idea
could be set
against
his fine-proportioned
muscles, his bronze shoulders?
There Time
opens its heart to everyone.

— 22 —

Through the unmown
grass
a girl walks.
Across the meadow
the blue-jays dive low.
I focus
to these sudden acts
which
capture my life like a wild animal,
and
I grow
so slowly
subdued.

24 | REMARKS to a DANISH PRINCE

Back to the beginning.
The beginning.
A chaconne played on the piano,
all the graceful steps
of the dancers.
Yes, I remember,
I remember everything.
In all the marble halls
and corridors
the people whispered in their fear
that they would vanish
on that night of ancient music
when the voices of the river
told us
it was only the beginning.

The sand
undulates across the dunes.

A beating
of birds' wings,
a force of wind, one
human syllable…
whatever breaks the silence
of the desert
is music.
In the valley
of the shadow of death,
one step of the wind
is music
slipping
out of the silence
which waits
at the sound's perimeter.

THE TREE AS A WORK OF ART

What grotesque dance
are the branches
of this tree,
twisted and wound
around
each other like human arms,
engaged in?
What are they
trying to communicate?
Above
the confusion of arms
and the choking leaves,
in the sky,
the plum blossoms
ride, a sea of white petals.

THE HOUSE THE DOZERS RAZED

Come in-
to my house.
You see where it stands.
The dogs
run over the hardwood floor
which now is grass,
a ball
sails through one window
and out another.
Come into my house,
my bed
hangs in the air
on the second floor,
and the balcony
with its double doors
tips into the camellias.
Come into my house,
the ceiling
is painted blue,
the walls are windows.
Come into my house.
I will not mind.
You see where it stands.
Come in-
to my house.

The shadows
of the trees
interlace on the ground.
A lattice.
In all these separate
boxes of shadows,
we pine
our lives away.
I will tell you what I mean.
I love…
I mean…
These squares of innocence,
mysteries,
suggestions.

A white-haired
woman
coming home from market.
In her clear
shopping bag,
the warm, yellow grapefruits
ride
like thimbles of the sun.
Slowly
she crosses her lawn,
opens her door carefully.
Her arm slips.
Happily the grapefruits
tumble out,
all together,
rolling down the steps,
out into the street,
far, far away.

ACHERON

On the riverbank,
the ferry
waits to leave.
The water
is as smooth as glass.
I take your hand,
and together
we watch our reflections
freeze like ice.
The boatman
with his long pole
throws
off the rope
and pushes away.
Across the river the rocks
are castellated
and rise like high columns
into the grey sky.
As the fog
gathers low over
the water,
a few curious souls begin to whisper.

Against
my naked chest,
a sword,
a cold blade of steel.
We lean
into each other
and balance
on the edge.
Whose hand is at the helm
my mind
does not see.

CINDERELLA

Numbers.
And where have you
slipped away to tonight?
You forgot
this slipper
(so warm in my hand
the inner sole)
at the threshold
of your door,
this glass slipper.
And so,
in my field of pumpkins,
I count my fingers
and wait.
I hope this wand is not
made of dust.

A Fresco of Ancient Etruria

The Etruscan singer
fingers
the strings
of his lyre of ivory
and horn.
Everything—
his scarlet robe,
his naked thighs,
his feet placed one before
the other—
is in motion with the music.
Only
his almond eyes
remain fixed and still,
perhaps
caught by the charm of accompanying
dancers;
perhaps,
more likely,
lost in that backward
flow of time
in which he lives,
where things grow younger
as they die.

On this hill
(which I have climbed
to watch
the sea)
the white butterflies
swim
through the tall grass,
dodging
here and there,
while
the wind invents
its
little games with the trees.

The Revolutionary Paintings of Goya

Where
did Goya store
the bloody limbs
of
all his half-eaten corpses?
The
carnivorous mouths
of his paintings
open
like tower doors
without stairs,
and you find yourself
falling,
falling,
falling.

MODULATION

I have not
seen you
for so long, so long.
All my wheels
begin to slow,
my limbs will not move.
O joy, joy!
Spikes of the sun
drive
like bullets
through yards of ice,
and I crack
wide open.

— 36 —

A Kind of Lazarus

O moth,
you blow through the air
in
random patterns
like an ash,
borne on your charcoal wings.
From
what return to flowers
and the stars
do you flee,
O remnant
of the fire and the flame?

I was led
to consider
the rocky coast,
and the way the sea
beat itself into foam.
And then,
how merciful
the rocks were,
as they let the water
wash
quietly off their backs,
or cradled it
in little pools
until the sea came back
again.

THE LANTERNS *in the* DARK FOREST

Even the ocean has its secret caves.

—R. GAJDUSEK

— 1 —

To be deprived of living
near the sea,
of the view of the water,
of horizons everywhere,
nowhere,
to live inland blind in both eyes
to everything
but the accessible patterns,
facing the clock in comfort:
but then, O
to burn in the sand,
to freeze in a sunless cave,
to be there
near the sea.

— 2 —

Later, much later,
I was gone.
In the mountains the clear air was thin,
I drove until exhaustion
left me white-faced,
weak in the face of danger
all around,
protecting what I still
was unprotected by.

— 3 —

Open!
The key, the lock, the gate
in the high fence
being
slowly
built
around me:
this the perimeter,
flowers crushed in the digging,
someone
consigned to disaster.

— 4 —

To achieve
(unmarred by what had seemed familiar)
the hearing
of the sound
of someone else's breathing
in the room.

— 5 —

Night-Fishing

The lanterns
in the dark forest
tremble
where brook and lake meet.
Silently
the spawning fish
ripple and dart
upstream.

"Yes, you see the view,
the Peaked Hill, the pond,
the valley and the mountains
far beyond."
And so I found myself,
utterly lost,
speaking to strangers,
the landscape
momentarily
caught in my bluff.

The mystery of heights—
arranging the peaks
in the distance—
here where the wind blows
in trees I will remember.
I have been thinking
of the heights
I have not seen, may never see,
Inca ruins,
Tibetan villages,
Caucasian monasteries:
where am I,
given over, blind,
thinking of the mystery of unknown heights?

To visit Venice as a child,
to tour the Bridge of Sighs,
descending the descending stairs
and subterranean corridors,
to watch, to see,
imagining unknown prisoners
sealed in their cells
(dark wells
of stone and putrefaction)
concealed with their offal,
bound by chains,
the last food refused,
the aperture sealed,
the body,
the body entombed.

He had come closer
to feeding
on the sustenance of mind,
the last rites,
precision
of self-encounters,
to view
all that painfully fell away
as his own,
the landscape he owned,
his own (refusal) to be.

Silent for so long,
my own intimate
one,
the voice is strange
to the ear,
lost in precaution,
threatening (strange to say)
disbelief,
with ear to the earth,
chest in the grass,
listening,
caught,
redeemed.

To be convinced
(stung by the will to be)
once and for all
that there is utterly
nowhere
but here,
here and now,
in the equations of time,
the matrix,
the depth
of possible
confrontations.

Wittgenstein: "Doubt
only when it is necessary
to doubt,"
that you are here,
that you are sundered
from ultimate paradise
and rain
glistening
on blades of grass.
Incorporate the heresy
to *be* (one and alone,
divorced from bliss,
the artery cut)
without hope
of ever attaining (pertaining)—
to give to the spilling of blood,
the hemorrhage within,
irreducible meaning,
atonement at last.

To be useless—
alone and alive,
to think to be useless,
(not
for the coin of compassion)
refusing
to keep up the effort
of being,
the dancing within.
Alone and alive.

STRICTLY OBJECTIVE

The tendency to cogitate,
the travesty of dream,
I labor to unravel thought
from what I guess is seen.
The last to come,
the last to go,
myself is caught between.
I excavate,
I operate
on objects heard and seen.

— 15 —
The Baptism

Granted
the irreplaceable pleasures
of touching, of being close and near,
of fondling,
of experimenting with hands—
granted all that,
what remains of ecstasy
to celebrate (to cerebrate)
except possibly, say,
discoveries of new stars
through telescopes
lovingly adjusted by hands too?

— 16 —

It was what I wanted,
the hazard
of harmony
held intact—
everything else I let fall away,
bequeathed
to the blind
what was wrongfully
mine.

— 17 —

The projection of precedence,
tradition—
to have suddenly
robbed
no vaults, stolen no treasures:
I wept
as the light
failed in my presence,
the room grew dim.

Beyond death—recovery.
Always an exile at heart,
I bandaged the wounds of seclusion,
considered the loss,
and spent what time remained
(strange eternity!)
feeling my way, touching my way,
from season to season,
man to man, city to city.
Beyond death,
where I harbored my dreams,
I came to believe in recovery.

I would not say—
I could not know—
what rank confusion
reigned—
death of the knowledge
of love
(abandoned, undefined)
unattended meetings
arranged
(in secret)
for lover and be-
loved.

To be disillusioned
with the mere festival,
the place, the time,
the perpetual outward
dispositions of things:
to want to celebrate,
to contemplate,
hermetically alone,
disprovable solutions,
differentiable renown.

In the country,
still perspectives of the moon,
observed (subserved)
through trees,
the dark distant silent forest.
To be a part of,
O, I am fled from it all,
consumed (subsumed)
by sheer fear of
unwillingness
to once and for all
partake.

Not to yield,
assuredly not to yield!
To live by the lake
for weeks
and finally
to unexpectedly see in the thick reeds
the blue heron
spread its wings
and fly
on a draft of wind,
at last to see that!
O I am fled (led) on my way,
(nowhere)
alive.

— 23 —

It is, yes, that one sees
the whole entire
intact
at once,
a fact,
nothing relinquished,
meridian given,
a possible venture,
forgiveness assured,
for what I deserve (serve)
I speak to you now.

The one and only way,
broken and blind,
gift of the stars,
broken away:
kind disaster fell
as was to be expected.
He lay by the road,
beaten and gouged
and avenged by fate,
too late
and for what?
(the innocent ask)

Thoroughgoing uncertainty—
redeemed
by the lord of the land:
exposed to the filtering sounds
of the morning.
Once more the sun
(selectively arranged)
decreed
reversed
anticipated fate.
It was the customary conclusion,
the return
from ravaging (night)
to utter, blind
and not so final
comprehension.

OPEN-HEART SURGERY

Before, during, and after,
nothing more:
the operation went like a dream.
I offered myself,
endured
cured
lured myself:
the scalpel dug to the bone.
For years it seemed
there was nothing to surgery,
nothing but this.
I willed it! I named it!
I answered
the dancer,
I spoke to the voice within!

Sing the dream songs,
sing realms of birth and death
(sing symmetry!)—
I followed far into the night,
precluded, concluded
the terms of the night.
O, I was here,
mysteriously here,
designed to discover the night.

Nowhere is the limit
of unbounded space,
everywhere the center of here.
I try to position,
I try to decipher,
I try to surrender to here.
The distance dissolved,
the time resolved,
I question the goddess,
(bereaved).

— 29 —

A calculation of attitudes—
how to hold a pose,
maintain a posture, a stance—
as when I glance
at (another) stranger
and
receive a strange response.
O, it is here
in the delicate pressure,
the battle of veils,
that someone is someone
indeed!

THE CONNECTION

Whispering,
going to the sacrifice (Who are these?)
it's more than skin-deep,
he said to himself,
receiver in hand—
the strange, electric crackling
of voices dis-
owned,
contusions of space.

Parenthetical Life

Symbolic wounds,
(the piercing of flesh)—
the premise no greater than that.
Dialectically phrased,
the answer was death,
the question exactly the same,
for though I reveled in masks
(the disguises were mine),
yet the end was wholly
design.

Meditation on a Steep Cliff

It was to be the last exhibition,
he proposed to himself
(surrounded by grass
to the knees):
but presented with mountains,
presented with sky,
he resumed in a trance
the invisible dance,
the limits of what he avowed.

The proposition
was not to discover
a placed in the sun,
a face
to reflect (deflect) the loss of his own,
but to edge by,
no more than survive
(not dive or thrive)
in the haunting
complexion
of darkening caves.

The touch—
to render,
to tender the throbbing.
He spoke with a quivering voice,
(to her—of sudden love,
barely, fairly alive).
The chances were slim,
the evening was dim,
as he gauged by the rim
of the moon.

It was over,
the encompassing fatigue,
the incomprehensible
intrigue
of bodies
perpetually moved, moving,
sights seen,
sounds sounding,
over,
over at last.

There.
Here.
Now
What?
Yes.
Oh!
Now
From.
Where?
To
Here.

TOMB (LOOM)

To have become
(alone)
the one and only witness,
of, by, and for himself,
he entered the door unseen:
Stark was the land (he saw) then,
dark unfurling dark,
his own one lost
and perishing instant of time (prime)
(bloom)
consumed.

Attendant upon
the wild woman
walking from town to town
at midnight
down the middle (riddle)
of the road,
he crossed wet streets
following (enraptured)
coincident
possible destinations.

Personified
preconditions of flight—
disguises,
investments of self,
the risks
incurred in the course of
(what shall I say?)
politeness,
the rightness
of masking each mood
where to give it away
would be asking
to slay (allay)
the temper, the tension,
the torrent within.

— 4 —

No one among those
not found there
(there being
no one lost there)
but listened well,
fell christened
from the silence there—
no one
at no invitation
(there being
no invitations there)
but knew elation
in relation
to the stillness there.

You of all people
from the steeple
I saw—
transfigured
in the lens of what
(that only perch
raw distance felt)
I saw,
believed,
received in whom
the image (of all people!)
I (the same)
became.

— 6 —

Till then,
nothing was known.
In, of all signals
crossed
lost
no meaning was seen
(the rhyme sublime,
the pattern,
the moment,
the dream
redeemed)
I—lost to the flow—
the blind
and perjuring
witness below.

Winter light—
I alone, not now,
if you could come
(if some could come)
to see
the clearness (nearness)
of the stars at night,
the distance,
cold, no distance,
not I, alone now,
far, near,
not I now fear
the pure vegetable
rotting within.

In the wind, of these,
I expressed a doubt
as to who (what)
should follow
in the wake
(the double take)
of my conspiracy
to live:
I—of all absences
I most prefer—
devised
revised
irreversible design—
not-I (to live)—
of all presences
I most defer—
(but what is given,
shriven)
blind, resigned.

So be it—
nothing from this moment on
but what I choose
to lose,
radiate (validate)
the confidence
of inference:
I—what I lose—
am, the sense
of the perishing,
ravishing,
putrefying
splendor of being,
decanter of darkness,
tomb (loom)
of the mysteries
of mirrors I am.

INTERLUDE

On the edge (ledge)
of the cliff,
I, he opened
my, his arms,
dove,
became
the terrific scream (dream)
of falling
into sky below,
warm wind
fell from the canyon
above,
I, he swirling,
trousers billowing,
fell out, free fall,
nowhere, desisting
insisting
I, he,
am,
is, was.

— 11 —

Someone on the fringe,
I there
to greet (entreat) her,
smile (beguile),
intimations
in the barren warren,
trees desolate,
transformations
of a fire on the land:
I exuberate
in that country
thus
(of reliques, ruined skeletons,
failing, blushing moon)

To capture
the rapture of—
no moment there
no blood,
I
among these things (rings)
wind, trees,
no rupture there
but I
the monumental
fundamental.

— 13 —

Silence
mathematically
conceived (believed),
I
in danger
from no stranger
except this self-
wrought,
self-abandoned distance,
quiet fury:
while
comparable concisions
(of decisions) made
fade
on parade.

— 14 —

In alliance held
by red sun (set
within the cleavage
of a hill)
and moon,
this tidal flow,
dance becoming
dance,
I speak
(intelligence
within the network
of the stars):
not one word fails
(prevails)
to render (tender)
my surrender.

The Ablative Absolute

Control of the pancreas
liver, spleen,
of this
I mean
the gift (rift)
of consciousness
where I
(subjective
in perspective)
drown
(frown
on self-indulgence)
in this deep sleep-
embracing.
coral-bedded,
blue black-
caverned sea.

But refuge…?
Whether, to represent oneself
refreshed (enmeshed)
in the encounter,
sun to sun
(the blazing shield
of confidence
that dominates the field)—
to calculate
immaculate conception,
envision expiration
in the fury
of possession
(burst the grape!) in rape
and plunder die
(and die again),

Or, conduct a truce
(in contemplation
of migration
through consecutive domains)—
in metamorphic mirrors
reflections
redefined
(Did I do that?
Am I responsible
for *that*?
trembling death-deceiver
asks)—
to withdraw
into the web
of silent
interstellar space,
he refines (defines)
himself aloof,
beyond the need of proof.

In the morning,
intersecting echoes
selecting space,
(listening
to Gabrielli's canzone)
voices
stone to stone intoned—
sun through
morning fog,
this truce
a long dream (it seems),
no fever
of love lost
between believer
and deceiver.

But to speak out—
the precedence
of evidence
for being alive,
gathered in listening—
these are the walls,
this the gate (fate)
where I deliberate,
no phony testimony
here,
I am myself,
a star a star,
this language
language written on the wall,
the presage
of a message
that—I heard you singing,
star to farther star.

SONG-CYCLE

My lungs were burning
in a dream,
my breath was thick with ash
(I felt the tension
of dimension
slowly slip away)
but when the body was consumed
(the flesh
but flakes of ash),
I then resumed,
I was exhumed,
the ash became a flower;
flower a tree,
tree a man,
the man a saintly dream:
I felt the fire kindle there,
I heard a voice
despair:
lungs were burning,
breath was ash,
but memory was learning.

There was no sky tonight—
I danced outside—
Capricorn and Cancer
were no answer
to an emptiness inside
(all animals were mine)—
O what a plague
to feel so vague!
(the goddess spurned me
with fatigue,
but she was part
of the intrigue)—
there was no sky tonight—
I danced outside—
(all animals were mine)

And this the sea—
(a ledge of rock
I stand upon).
If I could seize…
(a testimony
of disease
to want to calculate
appeasement so)
and this the sea—
(a flock of starlings
on the shore,
an island in the haze—
I watch it blaze)
a ledge of rock
I stand upon.

And if it were
because of her—
(the heart is torn
the body born)
I scratch my skin
with lusty grin
and I begin
to bleed
(O I am fed
these thighs outspread!)
And if it were
because of her—
(the heart is torn
the body born),
these the chains
and this the rock
(May sacrifice unlock!)

— 24 —

WINTER

An empty road,
the sun is out,
the wind like ice
against my cheek
(O I am weak!)
the poison flows
inside my clothes,
within my veins
it still explains
the dizziness I feel
(O how I reel!)
Is this a curse
I reimburse?
I cannot come,
I cannot go,
I see the lost blood
in the snow.

ELEVEN LYRICS, ONE PRELUDE

PRELUDE

Hope and honour-bound,
Every wave important
Leaving known land behind—
Expecting nothing   (but hard times)—
No man given over to illusions

Rushing into death:
Under angry water   (on burning sand):
She, the image and the cause,
Harbouring her secrets
Torn from knowledge   (of her passion born)—
Offering the chance
No man may dare refuse.

— 1 —

Pattern in an Open Field

How was it that we came
(twenty degrees
at midnight
and the frost upon your back…)
to that far corner
of the field?
(…as you got up
from where you lay
on frozen ground
and readjusted clothes
that after all
we were quite thankful for)
How was it that
to that far corner
of the field
we
thankful
came?

— 2 —

Life zones of lepidoptera,
(and I a recluse now,
pointing with bare arm
to patterns in the sky,
my climate
a geometry of stars
which I would show to you—
this cold night,
your cheek and ankle warm,
distinctly near)

— 3 —

The Poet Reflects Upon His Mistress

When dark
the water
in the pond
at evening falls
(and there are leaves
enough
to testify
to this)
how to account
for what
the sun composes
in reflections
which a leaf
(capriciously)
disturbs
and shatters
thus.

— 4 —

Still water
dark ground
now spring
(it was snowing
when you left,
ice locked
on the dancing pond,
raw branches
brittle
to the touch)

I have spent the day
alone
in meditation
with the blossoms
which are now (in May)
spreading petals
(I watched the rain today
adhere to them)
between the leaves
on branches
growing from the tree
which can be seen
beneath the window,
from the window
of your attic room,
while sitting
in your attic chair,
before the table
where there stands
a broken mirror, broken glass
(I see myself reflected in)

And so,
suddenly one dies
(in the night
a star
guides the happy man,
but still one dies)
You must believe me:
I would travel far,
leave suddenly
the pattern and the moment
which claim me
so completely:
so to die,
to live in deep
bestowal,
as I come to you.

Mist here—
in the valleys,
on the hills—
and this is far
(where sudden regions,
indentations
in the land
become,
the land
what I had known)
from where you are,
a country I create
and so inhabit
to the bone,
and all things
move
a man will dream until

So if you
please
to be
the stranger
(one
I had known
most closely),
I would range
to find you
among
what starkly
vindicates
my damaged sense
of loss,
the ecstasy
of turning
and the pleasure
of the eye.

You will think
I have
for other reasons
silence
kept
than
sun and shadow
on the lake
entrancing so:
bridges
lead me
where I go,
a song
is in the trees
ahead,
out of this
untamed
how it silence
always
onward
sings!

— 10 —

Now grass I see
and ferns[1] in clusters
by the walls,
(the winter was so long)
the brook
beside the house
is loud,
the waterfall is clearly
heard,
leaves slowly budding
slowly close
around the farther view
(in aching cold
I see you walk
across a snowy field,
deep dream of love
most closely held,
your breath
the only sign
of life
in air so hollow, deeply cold,
what takes
your breath away)

[1] *The Upland Lady Fern, Athyrium Filix-femina*

I bought you schedules,
saw you off,
was circumspect and brave:
how closely could I penetrate
my jealousy and rage,
my waiting and my watching
in a closely-guarded room?
I left you then in body
to return upon yourself:
less solemnly we take our way:
my touching of a leaf,
breathing of the air,
walking on the simple ground
give evidence, take memory
of my embracing you.

Nine Poems *in a* Boston Winter

On Leaving His Son At Nursery School

I watch him
from a distance
as he plays:
I've left him
for another day,
but linger
by an unimportant statue
on an island
between the traffic lanes
to watch him
on the playground
as he shyly
looks around
to find someone he knows,
and checks to see
I've gone:
we go our separate ways.

To Strangers Passing Underneath The Window Now

Nothing
in the paper
once again:
the stars are out tonight,
the wind is strong,
my wife and son
asleep.
City noises
are unusually
remote,
and I edge closer
to the night.
Then footsteps
on the street
three floors below.
One
never offers love enough
to strangers
passing underneath
the window
now.

To One Unsuccessful in Suicide

She rages in her room:
she's lost the pills again.
She gently weeps.
The doctors will not do.
The pots and pans
are full of dents,
the victims of her rage.
And you will not believe,
amid all this,
a drop of brandy
from my glass
has fallen on the page.

We cycled then
through half of Europe,
seeking shrines
and beaches too.
You rip the mirror
from the wall
and smash it
on the floor,
then praise your father:
he had courage,
so you say,
to go when it was time.
The doors they opened
easily,
the razor did its job.
What curse
upon the house
that nourished such a deed?

Still,
I have my books,
a shelter
from the wind
at night.
Occasionally
I laugh.
The window-glass
rattles
in the sash.
And yet my wife
sits up
through nights
and screams
she wants to die:
how deep
the springs of blood,
how cool the earth!

The day
I took you
to the hospital
I
was afraid:
all night
in the waiting room
you wouldn't speak,
your eyes
were locked in place:
a dismal table-lamp,
outside
the gentle rain.
Attendants came
to take you up:
I saw your face
pass behind
a window
in the elevator door.
Then silence,
the motor in the shaft,
and screams upstairs.

You vow to die.
Tonight
the nurses tell me
you tried to swallow
nail polish:
they had to lock you up.
I see you
on the mattress
in the Quiet Room.
They give you
an injection
to make you sleep,
at least
to keep you still.
The rooms
are much too hot,
centrally-controlled.
Outside
the snow accumulates
on dark earth and grass,
abiding roots:
the sky is falling.

Electro-Convulsive Therapy (E.C.T.)

I send you flowers
potted
wrapped in foil.
You ask why we are here.
The door
is open
to your room:
you suddenly recall
there's something
down the hall
you need:
you turn to go, but stop:
I watch your hands,
my empty hands.
You fall asleep.
I walk around the grounds,
cross a sidewalk
and a sheet of ice:
my shoes
are on their own.

Report and Search

The wind blows outside.
You are gone.
Police
have come
and taken names.
What grief,
steps upon the stairway:
it cannot be you!
Another room,
behind another wall
you plant
the poison
in your veins:
What melody of heaven,
dirge of love,
could urge
against the stillness
or the likely places
you might
in a multitude of numbers
choose
to go?

ELEGY

As I am in the room
within whose walls I saw you for the last time,
whose door (the door I open every morning now)
closed upon you as you left one winter night,
your smiling eyes, your hands
deceptively arranged inside the pockets of your winter coat,
then moving on the knob
whose door you were about to close,
as if suggesting something less disastrous
than what was then already formed and plotted
in the labyrinth where you had caught yourself
(dark, ancestral, through whose many turns
you doubled back many times confused)
something less disastrous
than that you would never reach the light of day again,
the wind across an open space of sun and light,
that you would never hear in wind the leaves of trees
caught and rustling, disturbed and then released,
taken up and given back, as is the way of wind and leaves,
that you would never step with firm intent
upon the ground, the earth, again,
would never feel the thrust
of bone and muscle and the impulse of the blood
as up along a mountain path you press your feet
against resistant earth and rock, in crevices of which,
despite the rock, bright flowers grow.

But there was in your blood a darker purpose,
which. we could not know, could not conceive,
was so attractive as to draw you down
beneath where even roots can thrive in conquest
of a land of dry, unyielding, universal rock.
Until the end you answered to the impulse of your blood.

And now I stand by open windows,
feeling on my hands and face a wind which blows
across an open space below: my feet are cold.
Shadows of the gulls and pigeons flying from roof to roof
weave patterns on the city streets, and on the grass,
and in reflections on a window now and then.
The children shout. I hear their many feet
beneath the trees inside the park, the drone of swings,
the metal links of chain against the metal bar
which holds aloft the swinger, whose knees
I glimpse between the leaves the wind has parted now:
I see the door, the windows and the room,
the walls which give us place
in which we may prepare ourselves, and greet
and say good-bye to those we love and wish to see,
and see again when once they've come and gone
and doors have closed once more.
What flower grows upon your breast (a dream of mine)
outside this room through which you passed, Persephone,
to darker earth?

THE PERSEPHONE SONNETS

Sonnet 1

Always as the stone is placed in pasture wall
Is strong the sun by how I close my eyes
Into the light as hard as is the ice
To fall upon or straight as wind may call
The tree: or tell that nothing less than all
The love you died for—wind against the rise
Of wind—could bring to cherished light (suffice)
A single stone in field in pasture wall.

In dark outside inside the light turned on
And every window gives me back my-
Self tonight a silent still intruder
Locking thought to thought: of you or why
You smashed the crystal night by night: incur
A love reduced to its essentials: gone.

SONNET 2

Portrait: you at midnight at your desk wine
The glass its curvature your hands that raise
In solitary concentration (phrase)
Your cigarettes your sleeplessness align
The words you pour out into journals line
After line seeking to explain the ways
Yourself becomes yourself the life that days
Accumulate and concentrate define.

And frost kills flowers leaves yes understand
To understand what happens how events
Both liberate and yet condemn us to
A pattern we fall victim to our planned
And open-ended Fate flowers trees currents
Of the wind follow into winter too.

SONNET 3

And winter: that year the ice was smooth clear
We skated nights voices even whispers
Halfway across the pond we could plainly hear
Against the wall of forest—it occurs
To me *our* voices too against the dome and brace
Of sky Orion rising intricate
And overwhelming above the space
Our voices build enclose and penetrate.

And then the ice that locks groans under pressure
Strikes fault lines a hundred yards—deep echo
Mysterious as Death-groan—I heard your
Blades scrap ice turn glide saw metal skates glow
Reflect the starlight on the ice You here
Beside me turn sweep by and disappear.

SONNET 4

I walked out late to visit you last night:
I had too much to drink reeled off into
The darkness slipped on ice my tipped feet flew
Out from under me: I banged my head: light
(Moon on clear snow) went out. My wristwatch tight
Was ticking in my ear as I came to
In still cold half-darkness: only trees you
In your hillside grave my ache Dawn's streaked light.

Life love go on: a tangled skein of bare
Branches black against the snow framed outside
The window: winter and the icy oak.
Today circling high rocks soaring a rare
Winter hawk: I watched wings warm bird breast glide.
I saw it from the window when I woke.

Sonnet 5

The message that I send will not surprise
Or startle you—I know now nothing could—
You will allow me to imagine good
Has come of rage and death tears sorrows sighs.
So young! Today wind whistles outside flies
The whirling snow: winter is deep in wood
On hill where once to watch your son you stood.
He speaks of you, is gentle sad and wise.

I too have gone my way: I've studied Greek
Collected butterflies, walked summer fields
Watched winter stars: you've now become part of
The wind sun rain snow stars light dark I seek:
These are the gifts, this is the earth that yields
Inescapable you here now Death Love.

SONNET 6

The birds have not come to our trees this year—
The cylinder of glass swings in the cold
Wind the full seed feast unfulfilled and old
And soggy waits beacons to birds not near,
They do not through the currents of air steer
Down their wings here, but huddled hidden fold
Their feathers do not venture are not bold.
I miss the darting wonder sudden fear.

But there's tranquillity in empty trees
Branches leafless swaying they bend click touch
The snow—then too *we* build and block
The space our empty space what we can seize
Composed of light we add to light, and such
Conceived relations sun tree hillside rock.

Sonnet 7

There is no use in waiting for what will
Or won't come: birds on other branches take
Whatever others give and others wake
In other places other rooms dark still.
And if the guests don't come or die we kill
Time thus. But your anxiety? At stake
You made it clear was Life itself—to wake
At dawn a tranquil lake no ripples break.

I hurry through the woods: *this* was the path
We took. Look, a branch you broke! There's
Your bootprint in the snow! You died before
What came to meet you in its joy or wrath
Cut out the ground from under you. Who dares
To follow where the steps lead out the door?

Sonnet 8

And into April birds lift sheer blue sky
As Rilke said: the day is windy mild.
I stay inside read lie in bed beguiled
By you not here: I think of you I try
Not to think of you not think, my thoughts filed
To a too fine edge: "here" "not here" unstyled
By any but the desperate chasm "Why?"

What words will do for you for me? I came
To learn from you though your heart flared then froze
In its cage of rage: nerved reluctant proud.
You would not take give a light kiss the same
But bit the lip and bled. Nor would the rose
Decline—your smile half-understood—its shroud.

SONNET 9

And flowers then in spring early April
The fields above the Susquehanna you
Drove from Washington to meet me: winds blew
Warm in the afternoon overcast still:
On back roads we found a fresh-cut field full
Of the mown smell of hay and into
It we walked lay thighs together sky blue
Turning in the haze your body arched still.

Then down below the clump of willow trees
A wagon worked its way across the slope
Men were baling we could still naked hear
The creak of axles wheels our lovesweat breeze
Was forehead cooling lay and listened grope
We did our hands through broken grassblades near.

SONNET 10

Your last night you cooked the dinner left went
I thought to one more doctor's appointment.
Your smile was tranquil and your eyes assured
A week before you said that you were cured.
I put our son to bed then watched the clock
You did not come I waited felt the shock
Of city noises sirens sudden light
Unknown calamities of secret night.

And ours was one alone your secret too,
So no more doctors hospitals false hopes
The autumn in Jamaica Plain bleak brick
Buildings blank stark wards bleached white gowns for you
Shock therapy and doctors doctors slopes
Of oak trees leaves Jamaica Pond Lovesick.

And I will come to know this long sleep too.
A month before you died we laughed in bed
In Mexico—you gave me love you led
Me to the ache of love sweet darkness knew.
City lights adjacent rooms warm wind blew
In palm trees on the avenues—you said
It had to end but laughed drew close: we read
Our books. I thought Death would not conquer you.

Swiftly swiftly Sleep came and Love was closed
As was the door through which you passed—the night
You entered driving north toward the village:
Childhood Marriage Death there, and you disposed
Of agony sweet Sleep dispersed the light
The last dread vestiges put out of rage.

Sonnet 12

So on to other things. I think of friends
And you—your smile—peninsulas the land
Near San Francisco you the hot white sand
Of California shore where the coast bends
Into Bodega Bay, a road that ends
Where grassland ends cliffs fall and boulders stand
On the beach in eddying swirls—your hand
Points out to sea—a pelican descends.

You loved to read there on a rock Camus,
The spray would wet your hair—you'd read, confide:
There's only one truly serious (too)
Philosophical problem: Suicide.
This was the problem you set out to solve.
And Love is difficult—ourselves involves.

SONNET 13

Not you but places strange cities stark
The feeling gone the struggle to recall
What angered you or made you smile: the fall
And crash of something precious in the dark.
In Paris once we lost a hotel key (park
Lights dim below) we pressed against the wall
And listened to our breathing in the hall.
Who listened then behind the doors blank stark?

Useless these words bright scarves connect: in dreams
You stand behind a darkened door ajar
Or in a shadowed wood—I squint stare strain
Or simply stand perplexed and wait—it seems
I wake: your hands, held out, a flash afar
Of light caught offered Death cannot explain.

Sonnet 14

Lady you are inside my heart a sweet
Wound, come and gone the suitor Death: I taste
The bitter fruit. And you? You turn and turn
On lovely earth this dance in space you learn
Though you are gone to ground and no repeat
Of tears can bring or song can ring you faced
With darkness blinded gracefully displaced
From sadness Love your fury too back Sweet.

Given me now is Time condolent kind
To hold encompass you while silence throbs:
In thought (a curse on thought!) our paths how crossed
Now seem and you to death: you could not find
A more effective thief who bitter robs
You dancing on the bright ground opened lost.

Sonnet 15

To speak to you my language syntax not
Avail me now what even I declare
Allege my heart reduces to despair.
But spare! yes I *can* tell such a key got
I *do* know such a place: Love survives the knot
Of places things you've lived among: the care
Entrusted me that you become what there
You've given Beauty of yourself shared kept not.

For nothing else abides: your death confused
Your clothes still in boxes in the attic
Coats blouses skirts slips nightgowns underwear
Rain on roof we heard smelled the room we used
To sleep in in your mother's house the prick
Of Love the wet wood-fragrant attic air.

Sonnet 16

How painful then to see the vanity
Of other women dresses mirrors hair
Arranged bold laughter love how *could* they care!
Adjustments in the stockings at the knee
Smoothing of the pleated skirt symmetry
Of eye to eye hip to hip what breasts wear.
So no one knows of you! Talk dream love stare
The seasons pass singing wind is cold free.

And all arranged as table-flowers Fate
What could you possibly be guilty of?
Herself a fairer flower by gloomy Dis
Was plucked: and people grow from darkness mate
Die in darkness fear hope grieve lament miss
The trees the singing wind you passing Love.

SONNET 17

And words words explanations of the thing
Your body had become the web that it
Had spun around itself adjustments fit
That you might understand: but what could bring
A clearer focus final silencing
Of words failing? The problems we admit
Life solves according to its need: our wit
Or others' Death explains escape or cling.

Bright flowers in the fields are cut become
Ornaments: we remember light in dark:
The overwhelming Fate approaching you
Your words (I read them now) could not avert or numb
Ironically express accept stark-
Ly nakedly fulfil encircle you.

Sonnet 18

In deep woods through autumn the cold trees sing
Chill winds cut clear beginning as we hear
See the house lights dark nights alone appear
Across St. Lubin's Pond the sudden sting
Of icy water grips the ankles wing
Migratory birds south ducks hunters deer
The Great Blue Heron crooked wings aloft near
Shore reeds apples pressed pumpkin harvesting.

And trees contusions of the leaf the wind
Spins off the branch scatters sweeps swamp maple
Scarlet crimson oak bronze ash gold poplars
Birch yellow sumac fire-red opened
Against the rustling wind-sonata full
Then down Capella Taurus clearer stars.

REMARKS *to a* DANISH PRINCE

REMARKS TO A DANISH PRINCE

Turn, and turn again,
                    and always
there is Fortinbras, a spectre rising
above the horizon, approaching
like a distant bright reflection,
hauberk and helmet fit into proper
position, the strong arms widening
an invincible path before the invisible foe.
He places history behind
his bright column marching across
the plains—ravished and set
in final, indestructible patterns.
He disdains whatever language you would speak,
what words you choose; he fastens
in his eyes the steel that would answer,
should he so will, your own
                    delicate

observations.

To This Day, This and No Other (Easter 1971)

To this day, this and no other,
to an afternoon of conversation with relatives
in sunny backyards, wrought-iron furniture,
a glass table, an oak's branches
twisted in meticulous directions
and counter-directions overhead,
to enter into the faces arranged in smiles
and red cheeks, anticipating,
as if expecting a concert to begin,
to expect the music yourself,
to anticipate your anticipations.

To this day, this and no other,
to feel the way a sweater creases when you bend
your arm, to absent-mindedly agree
when someone suggests it's cold outside,
but to be thinking of the grass and sky,
of nothing in particular,
an airplane, the resurrection,
to discuss current topics in the news,
and walk before dinner, already aware
of the first effects of the wine,
to concentrate precisely on your shoes.

To this day, this and no other,
to speak with the tension of having nothing
to say, to laugh for no reason and draw
quizzical stares, to slip
from your chair and fall in the ivy,
and have the dogs think you want to play with them,
to become cold, to say good-bye,
to navigate your way home
on the freeways under the stars,
to sleep the fullness of sleep,
to this day, this and no other.

Suicide on the London-Cambridge Railway

Did he master all the necessary moments
Of the act minutes
Before the arrival, walking across
The wide fields and up to the track,
Fixing his visions and all the day's
Diverting images before
The one ubiquitous mirror, adjusted
And set for every field of sight?

We pass unnoticed through miles of countryside;
Within our speed, one smooth, devouring
Act resides, seen by no one,
As my lungs expand to catch unknowingly
The intoxicating breath
Of flesh burning beneath our feet.

All in an instant, the shattering of a structure
Of mirrors, and the fields behind
Opening in naked brilliance:
We stop, compelled to consider
His movements in disbelief;
He conjures for our minds in strict detail
The moments of the fields
Passing before our unregarding sight,
And speaks, as all our lives,
Against the fact of his own death.

The Opera Singer Who Lives Across the Street

The opera singer who lives across the street
keeps the skeletons of two cars
in the vacant lot by his house.
A telescope he built himself points its nozzle
at the heavens above a palm tree,
which waves its head as if rehearsing
for an aria's soprano part.
A sailboat on its trailer is parked out front;
it has not sailed this year, but stands
like a varnished music box full of sea melodies.
Through the unmown grass a grey-haired friend
in a sweatshirt goes hopping about like a rabbit;
a family of dogs plays house by the cellar door.
These are the notes of wisdom
moving back and forth across a river gorge
whose bridge is built of the finely-threaded vocal chords
of the opera singer who lives across the street.

SONG OF THE BUTTERFLIES

Happy, happy the thronging of the butterflies,
orange and black their gossamer wings
lift to the wind, and are lightly blown

like so many leaves from a butterfly tree.
Is it earth or is it sea?
Is it meadow, field or valley?

Is it summer? is it winter? is it autumn? is it spring?
Is it day or night, dawn or what?
Listen, and you hear the butterflies sing:

Turn and turn, we lead no more the lives we led,
shell or skin or bark or fur,
the wind is all the body we need.

The trees are floating up and down,
the wind is here, and then the wind is there,
O is it up, or is it down? is it here or is it there?

Is it sun or moon? is it late or is it soon?
Orange and black our gossamer wings
lift to the wind, and are lightly blown.
Tell us, O Wind, do we live or do we die?

To My Brother-in-Law,
Going to Cuba to Cut Sugar-Cane

To free the present from the past.
—Regis Debray

The taste of things to come will be better.
The salt of a man's sweat is the salt of the earth,
though a few thousand stars fall
and crash in the fields like faulty airplanes.
Tomorrow you will push the black stones of memory
into the sea, into the curling lips of the sea:
the fine spray flies in your face
like morning with a fresh and friendly slap.
The sun invents a host of new expressions
in the natural world, beating a slow drum over the soil's hide.
The arms of all brothers
are intertwined in the arms of their brothers,
and heavenly feet raise dust on the road
for miles ahead, the sinuous, film-like dust of mirage.
Bring back the news from Cuba,
from the sugar-cane fields,
"they are raising Jerusalem across the river,"
across the river where the mind
drops off the edge of the flattened world,
while here we strip the centuries off the spherical walls.

Skiing in Sierra Nevada

This land of echoes we gra-   rise
                      dually a-
into, surpassing higher levels
                         of silence, ascending
to the snow so clear
                 that all contours
dis-
    appear against the imperishable sky: we re-
cede into that sphere
                    of only our own thin wake dis-
turbing the thought of the snow,
                     as we reappear over
the steep face of the mountain,
                      maintaining a delicate
balance for the spiraled des-
                cent to the valleys
below.

Going to Sleep

In the darkness I am a free-fall diver,
blacking out as I jump farther, farther into the night.
Nothing remains of the gold adornments,
clothes, leaves, lines and squares of light,
the way I rearrange the sun,
as if plotting it on the graph of life.
Familiarity sheds its skin, like a writhing snake
that leaves behind a scale-like ghost
of itself, thin as filament.
Where has the body gone?
Where do the crepuscular walls that are opening lead?
The projections of my sight are like divining rods.
Away, away! The loudest sound is quietness,
the quickest feet are still.
A hand like the sky lightly brushes my eyelids.

THE POET'S SONG: PART I

I was with Socrates in the court at Athens
I was an attendant in the palace at
   the coronation of Charlemagne
I stood with Roland and Oliver at Roncevalles
I listened to Bernard on the hill at Vezelay
I was Tristan who came to Cornwall and to Ireland
And killed the Norholt and won Iseult
I heard Abelard and Meister Eckhardt
I knew the Rose and every good man in Aquitaine
And left to fight in every border war
I came to Francis on the Loire and read
And measured out the cloth turned out with gold
Two hundred years later for the Sun King's Court
I slept at Hampstead when the light
Was burning late in Keats' window
And saw the boat go down from the Ligurian shore
   when Shelley died.
I trimmed the vines at Muzot under the walls
Where Rilke came to write the Elegies and Sonnets
And dug the grave at Raron
And later too for Yeats under Bare Ben Bulben's Head.

The Poet's Song: Part II

There was horizon's level plain:
I stepped and smote the sand with hooves
And knew the sky and burning sun,
To build in drifts a firmer ground
And raise a city to be seen,
By flowers in the desert bloom.
I could conceive, I did remit
The whirling vision of the brain,
And gave my hands direction true
To calculate the shapes I knew,
By whom, by what I could conduct
The fruits of what my people struck,
In furrows or in deeper mines
Recall to light what light defines.

We gave a shape to what we found
Though many slept a deeper sound
Than dancing what we trembled down
In forest, village or in town:
Cold nights, dark days, we grew to love
The passion we were master of.

Greek Choral Fragments

Ω ΖΕΥ ΒΑΣΙΛΕΥ   Zeus King   ΚΑΙ ΝΥΞ   Night

Friend   Keeper of Great Worlds   (stars

         gliding planets and the moon)

Night   for You it was

          cast

On Troy's towers

       over roofs   Darkness

A covering net

     ΝΥΞ   that neither old nor young

Leapt up   nor could escape

         the mighty drag-net

ΓΑΓΓΑΜΟΝ   sweeping the caught

         to slavery

(Death and Drudgery)

         Doom that catches all alike:

ΔΙΑ ΞΕΝΙΟΝ   Zeus   Friend of Strangers

         Greeting of the Guest and Host

I hold in awe   Who   only He

Accomplishing   has done

         long since bending

His bow at Alexander

       aiming

The shaft he lets fly

      through Time foreknown exactly

Threading ΚΟΣΜΟΣ

underneath the stars   on target   its way

To hit the mark

        predestined.

Choral Fragment 2: Agamemnon [367]

Loud-ringing   the stroke of Zeus

          ΔΙΟΣ ΠΛΑΓΑΝ

      Strike of Doom,

Of this

     it can be told,   tracked out,   the

consequence

Is known.   Done as He ordained.

           Ungodly

The One who claims   ΟΥΧ ΕΥΣΕΒΕΣ

         gods forget

Overlook

     the trampling underfoot of things

untouchable

And violated Grace.

      Through generations   Zeus

Remembers,

     the Penalty devolves

Though devious   direct

       exacts its toll

Punctures swollen Pride

     Audacity,   and Houses

Teeming with abundance

      shears to Nothing.

So that for those

     with Understanding

Sound and tested,

    it suffices to be free

Of Sorrow   Misery.   They ask no more.

ΜΕΓΑΣ ΔΙΚΑΣ ΒΟΜΟΝ
Great Altar of Justice
                 honor.
For him who in the glut of wealth
        kicks into Darkness
This
        No Protection.

ΠΕΙΘΩ   She   Persuasion
                      Who compels, relentless,
Irresistible,   Child of ATH—
                    Sheer Destruction,
Insinuating plots and schemes
                         enticements,
Infatuation
              for which all remedies are pointless
And the consequences known,   shines forth
And
       terrible the brightness of the light,
                          Calamity,
Not hidden,   done.
                As bronze impure, beaten,
Rubbed,
       is blackened,   thus
Tested,   known.
             So a boy runs after a winged bird   ΕΠΕΙ
ΔΙΩΚΕΙ ΠΑΙΣ ΠΟΤΑΝΟΝ ΟΡΝΙΝ

Has laid on his people,
               city,   unbearable affliction.
No god will listen to his prayers,
                    but yanks
Him down,
        unjust,   condemned.

And such was Paris
        come
From the Atreidaen
        House,
          dishonouring
The offered hospitality
          of lodging   table shared
By Helen's theft.

Choral Fragment 4: Agamemnon [404]

                                        Once gone

She left behind

                    a Clamour   Clash of shields

Assembled warriors

                       sailors armed for battle:

This bride   no dowry hers   but Death

       Destruction

Brought to Ilium.

                       She dared what no one dared,

Was gone   so lightly   through the Gates,

And

        all the prophets in the Palace groaned:

IΩ   IΩ   ΔΩMA   ΔΩMA   KAI   ΠPOMOI

O God

          God   the House   the House,

                            our Princes

too,

The Love her footsteps

                    brought her Lord

When thus

        she came to bed at night.

                             And

Menelaus stares in silence now

                  like all forsaken men,

We see it now

        an empty silence   no Honor

No Abuse,

cannot believe that She is gone

Across the Sea.

And Longing,   longs for

Her

And

it will seem   her Phantom   rules the House

ΦΑΣΜΑ   ΦΑΣΜΑ   ΔΩΜΑ   ΔΩΜΑ

All lovely statues now

despised,

Of Love, of Her Reminders

In the hollow stony Eyes

That Aphrodite's

gone.

Choral Fragment 5: Agamemnon [420]

In Dreams appear the Visions

ΟΝΕΙΡΟΦΑΝΤΟΙ

Caught with grief

and bearing bitter Joy—

We see the faithful lovely Form

Of one who once was dear,

in vain,

for

What we think we see   so quickly slips aside

Between our hands,

the Vision gone

ΦΑΣΜΑ   ΦΑΣΜΑ

ΩΠΙΣ

not afterward   to follow

On its wings   down

Paths of Sleep.

Such the Sorrows

Menelaus feels beside the Hearth.

And others too, surpassing these.

In every House, of every Man

who sailed for Troy

A woman's heart

enduring   mourns.

ΑΧΗ   Sorrows   everywhere.

Somehow it gets to you.

ΠΟΛΛΑ ΓΟΥΝ ΘΙΓΓΑΝΕΙ ΠΡΟΣ ΗΠΑΡ

The men they sent to war

They know;

Instead of men

Come back

The urns and ashes

ΤΕΥΧΗ   ΣΠΟΔΟΣ

Empty   empty   House.

Choral Fragment 6: Agamemnon [437]

Ares   Gold-Changer   of bodies
            Ο ΧΡΥΣΑΜΟΙΒΟΣ   who holds aloft
The Scale
            in battle where spears fly
(And weighs out corpses turned to dust)
            What has been burnt
From Ilium
            home to kinsmen   sends,
                        the heavy dust,
What's left   of bodies
                  ΨΗΓΜΑ
To bitter weeping comes
                  ΔΥΣΔΑΚΡΥΤΟΝ
Loading urns
            for passage   on the ships,
Stowed with ease
                  (more so than men)
Ashes—
            Men no longer.
                        They take the ashes,
Kinsmen,   groan   lament,
                        the battle-skill of some
They praise,
                  and others   honorably dead
      in Slaughter   Praise.
But dead for what?
                  Another man's wife!

They snarl   and whisper   thus,

                            their grief, resentful,

Spreads   in secret

                            for the Leader's War.

                Others there along the Wall

                Tombs of Ilian Earth

                      ΘΗΚΑΣ ΙΛΙΑΔΟΣ ΓΑΣ

                ΕΥΜΟΡΦΟΙ   occupy.

                   The Hated Land

                They fought to win,   Possessed,

                      Is now their Crypt.

Choral Fragment 7: Agamemnon [456]

Heavy   is the People's talk

                       with Anger now:

It pays the debt   the People's Curse,

                    brought down, exacted.

We dread

          to hear of what could happen now

ΝΥΚΤΗΡΕΦΕΣ

          What Darkness hides.

                       Not unregardful

Are the Gods   ΟΥΚ

          ΑΣΚΟΠΟΙ   ΘΕΟΙ   of Killers, Butchers,

Those who shed unnecessary Blood.

                  And Dark Furies

ΚΕΛΑΙΝΑΙ   Δ   ΕΡΙΝΥΕΣ   in Time

          wear down the Life

             unjustly prospering,

                  Calamities

Obliterate.   Unseen.   No Help.

          To be well spoken of,

               extravagantly praised,

Is a heavy thing to bear:

          Zeus sees,

               he hurls

          His Thunderbolt.

I choose a simple Happiness,
　　　　No Envy there.
No Sacker of Cities
　　　　ΠΤΟΛΙΠΟΡΘΗΣ
Nor Prisoner may I be,
　　　　But see
My Life not someone else's,
　　　　But my own.

ΑΡΙΣΤΟΝ ΜΕΝ ΗΥΔΟΡ

Water is best

And Gold

like Fire blazing   in the night

Ο ΔΕ ΧΡΥΣΟΣ   ΑΙΘΟΜΕΝΟΝ   ΠΥΡ

Shines out   conspicuous

above all lordly wealth.

And if to sing

of Prizes

Is your wish,

dear Heart,

Give up the search

for any shining star

By day   ΘΑΛΠΙΝΟΤΕΡΟΝ

more warming

through the desolate Sky

than Sun,

Nor let us praise   a Festival

more renowned than Olympia.

From there,   the famous Hymn

is cast   like a net

Round the thoughts

of poets   thinking men

ΟΘΕΝ Ο ΠΟΛΥΦΑΤΟΣ   ΗΥΜΝΟΣ ΑΜΦΙΒΑΛΛΕΤΑΙ
                                    ΣΟΦΟΝ

ΜΕΤΙΕΣΣΙ

So that   they loudly sing

                                the Son of Cronos

When they come

                        to the rich and blessed Hearth
                        of Hieron,

Choral Fragment 9: Olympian Ode 1, Antistrophe A

Who   wields with reverence

                  the Sceptre

Of the Laws   laid down

                  by Custom and the Gods

        ΘΕΜΙΣΤΕΙΟΝ   ΣΚΑΠΤΟΝ

In Sicily   where trees are rich in fruit

        ΕΝ ΠΟΛΥΜΑΛΩΙ   ΣΙΚΕΛΙΑΙ

Gathering   the blossoming   crowns

                  of Excellence.

And bright   he's made,

        Renowned,

In the Flower

        of Music   Poetry,

While many times

        Around the festive Table

We Men   dance and sing.

But take down

                              the Dorian Lyre

ΔΩΡΙΑΝ   ΦΟΡΜΙΓΓΑ   from its peg,

                                                  if

Grace   and   Beauty

                              in Pisa and Pherenicus

Have   truly   affected   you,

                              laid under the spell

Of   sweetest   Thoughts

                              your Mind: that time,

Beside the Alpheus

                              the horse's lovely body

Galloped by,

                              no spurs were in his side

The length   the race-course ran,

                              But for his Master

                                        Victory attained,

The horse-loving Lord of Syracusa
        ΣΥΡΑΚΟΣΙΟ   ΙΠΠΟΧΑΡΜΑΝ
ΒΑΣΙΛΗΑ
For Him   Glory
        ΚΛΕΟΣ   shines
                in the bravely-
manned colony
Of Lydian Pelops,
        with whom the mighty Earth-Shaker
ΓΑΙΑΧΟΣ   Poseidon
          fell in love,
When   Clotho
        lifted him out of the cleansing cauldron,
One shoulder   gone,
      replaced,   given the gleam of ivory.
Η   ΘΑΥΜΑΤΑ   ΠΟΛΛΑ
       Yes,   Wonders are many,

                                  and

As for the Tale   told among Men,

            ΔΕΔΑΙΔΑΛΜΕΝΟΙ   ΜΥΘΟΙ

Stories cunningly   laced   perhaps

                          with glittering lies,

     deceive,

Cut   through

            the Truth.

ΧΑΡΙΣ

Transforms all things   for men,

soothes,

Brings Honor

ΚΑΙ   ΑΠΙΣΤΟΝ   ΕΜΗΣΑΤΟ   ΠΙΣΤΟΝ
ΕΜΜΕΝΑΙ

and often   cunningly   contrives

to make

The Unbelievable

believable:

But Days To Come

ΗΑΜΕΡΑΙ   Δ   ΕΠΙΛΟΙΠΟΙ

Are the most reliable

Witnesses.   And it's best

for Men

To say   good   things   about the Gods

ΑΜΦΙ   ΔΑΙΜΟΝΩΝ   ΚΑΛΑ.

the Guilt,

The Consequences,

are less severe.

Son of Tantalus,

I won't sing about you

as the Poets have before,

But differently,

that time   your Father,

in exchange

For the Banquets he had attended,

                             invited the Gods

To his own   Feast   lawfully arranged

                                    at Sipylus,

And Poseidon   of the Bright Trident

                 ΑΛΓΑΟΤΡΙΑΙΝΑΝ

                               snatched you

away,

Choral Fragment 12: Olympian Ode 1, Antistrophe B

ΔΑΜΕΝΤΑ   ΦΡΕΝΑΣ   ΙΜΕΡΩΙ

                Poseidon,   broken

                          with

Love,

        demented,

In his golden-horsed Chariot

                carried you off

Up to   the   highest House

                  of widely-

honored Zeus

        ΕΥΡΥΤΙΜΟΥ   ΔΙΟΣ.

There   in later times

                  Ganymede came too,

Brought by Zeus

              for the same reason.

And when you were out of sight

        ΩΣ   Δ   ΑΦΑΝΤΟΣ   ΕΠΕΛΕΣ

              and the men

Who looked all around for you

              brought nothing

back

To your Mother,

              no sign of you,

Some   jealous neighbors

              soon began to spread the

word

        secretly

They cut up   your limbs

                                    with a knife

Into water   fired

                        to the pitch of boiling,

And around the tables

                        the last bits   of your flesh

ΔΙΕΔΑΣΑΝΤΟ   ΚΑΙ   ΦΑΓΟΝ

                        divided up

                                    and ate.

ΠΟΛΛΑ   ΤΑ   ΔΕΙΝΑ
                              Many   the strange things—
Yet
              Nothing   stranger than Man
                                        who voyages
The white-capped sea   in storms   the South-wind blows,
Through swells
                        engulfing.
                                                  ΓΑΝ
Oldest of the Goddesses
                                    Mother Earth
Imperishable
                              inexhaustible   He wears away
As ploughs go back and forth
                                    year in   year out
The furrows   churning Earth
                              beneath the brood of
horses'
Hoofs.

Flocks

          of light-dreaming birds

                              soaring

He hunts,   and the animal herds

          of the fields

And the sea-swelling   salt-water creatures

With woven nets

               encircling

          ΠΕΡΙΦΡΑΔΗΣ   ΑΝΗΡ

          Man   of   Encircling   Thought,

He masters   by his Arts

               ΜΑΧΑΝΑΙΣ

          (Contrivances)   the beasts

That   mountain-roaming

                    live in fields:

The shaggy-maned horse he tames,

                    puts under the yoke

The mountain-haunting

                    never-tired bull.

CHORAL FRAGMENT 15: ANTIGONE [354]

ΚΑΙ ΦΘΕΓΜΑ ΚΑΙ

ANEMOEN

ΦΡΟΝΗΜΑ   And Language   and

wind-swift

Thought   and the impulse

to live together,

Bind himself to cities,   laws,

He has developed,

taught himself,

And Shelter

from the piercing frost

its arrow's bite,

The   cold   clear   air

and stormy shafts of rain.

ΠΑΝΤΟΠΟΡΟΣ

Who finds a passage everywhere,

Resourceful Man:

ΑΠΟΡΟΣ   ΕΠ ΟΥΔΕΝ ΕΡΧΕΤΑΙ

passageless

He comes upon   nothing

that is to be.

but makes his way.

ΑΙΔΑ   Death   alone

blocks all escape:

No passage there.

But   Anguish   Sickness

                           baffling Disease,

From these,

         Escapes   He has devised,

                 thought out.

Subtle   wise
                    resourceful in his Skill,
With technical expertise
                              beyond belief,
Sometimes   He meets Calamity,
                    sometimes things   turn out well.
ΤΟΤΕ   ΜΕΝ   ΚΑΚΟΝ ΑΛΛΟΤ ΕΠ ΕΣΘΛΟΝ ΕΡΠΕΙ
When
                He weaves together
                              the Laws of the Land
And the   sworn   justice
                              of the Gods
                    ΥΨΙΠΟΛΙΣ

High   is   the city then,   pre-eminent and proud
                Is He,   the Citizen.
                                        But
ΑΠΟΛΙΣ   without a City   He
                              who dares dishonor
                Laws and Justice.
Never may I share my hearth,
                              or inner thoughts,
With him who does these things
                              ΟΣ ΤΑΔ   ΕΡΔΟΙ.

The Seafarer

From the Anglo-Saxon

The Seafarer

True words from myself   may I awake and sing
to speak of journeys,   how I suffering

5   sailed afflicted,   what endured.
while bitter breast-cares   bore within.
I knew in ship   sorrows many,
awesome, whelming waves.   The watch I kept
about the prow,   plunging ship

10   through darkest nights   the dark cliffs loomed above.
Cold were my feet   in frost-chains fast.
Fervent thoughts   thoughts unforeseen,
laid siege my heart: hunger lanced within
sea-weariness.   Suffice to say

15   the man who fares   most fortunately on land
can never know   nights I knew,
paths of exile,   exile-vows I held,
wretched on the icy sea,   winter biding there,
hung with hoarfrost.   Hail in showers flew.

20   There heard I nothing   but the howling sea,
its icy waves;   at times imagined,
mad suggestions,   swan's and gannet's songs
and curlew's cry   crazed laughter-cries of men,
wail of seagull mourning   mead-drink lamentation.

25   Storms there the stonecliffs beat   where strikes
the echo of the tern: ice-feather-winged,
and scream of eagle   soaring
damp-feather-winged.   Dear blood-companions
could not cheer   my cheerless spirit then.

30 And so the man who bides   the blessings of life
    in safety of his dwelling,   death-risks
    and adversaries few,   wine-flushed, exulting,
    cannot comprehend   that I continue,
    must abide   my exile on the sea.
35 Night's shade grew dark,   from the north it snowed,
    hoarfrost bound,   hail fell on earth.
    Cold harvest that!   Thoughts of the heart
    beat boldly now: beyond the cliffs
    to the open seas,   the salt-wave surge,
40 thoughts drive me out: what's death to me?
    Longing of the spirit   leads me now
    to journey far,   and far from here,
    a pilgrim's calling,   pursue a pilgrim's home.
    Truly on earth is not a man   so magnificent and proud,
45 so bold in youth   and brave in deeds,
    so generous in gifts,   to whom so gracious is the Lord
    that he on sea-journeys   has not a second thought
    for what the Lord   allots to him.
    On harp does not reflect,   on ring-receiving ponder,
50 he contemplates nor wife   nor worldly joy,
    but rivets thought   on rolling of the waves.
    And always he leaves   land for sea
    whose longing   lures him there.
    Woods take flowers   fields grow fair,
55 dwellings adorn the land: life goes on.
    Death-cycles these, they urge   the eager spirit on

to journey on flood-ways,   far to fare,
a pilgrim's calling   pursue a pilgrim's home.
Summer's guardian,   sad cuckoo sings,
60   summons sorrow: soon fruit ripened falls.
That's bitter keeping   in the breast,
bitter treasure,   yet it's true:
Nothing lasts!   No man can know,
self-satisfied,   how suffer some self-exiled,
65   wandering widest,   yearning yonder.
But now my spirit's hopeful: high and far
I feel it fly   from out my breast:
it wanders earth's expanses,   whale's abode,
the sea, the flood,   and full of longing
70   ravenous returns.   "Regard," it cries,
"the way to God!   The way that's irresistible!"
I contemplate that way: more crucial
is to me, more fervent too,   fire of the ecstasy
of dwelling close to God,   than this dead life
75   borrowed here on land.   Do not believe
earth's treasures   truly time outlast.
Always man must die,   and doubts arise
before life's done: disease, old age,
sword-hatred in a war: which one will work
80   to force life   from fated ones,
those doomed to die,   departure-due?
All man may hope   is heartfelt praise
in after-days   when death has come,
praise of the living,   of last-words the best:
85   therefore should work   before his way he takes,
good deeds on earth   against his enemies,
bold feats outfacing   all false gods.

Then may the sons of men   sound praises afterwards,
in glory afterwards   with Angels may he live.
90   Forever may he breathe   breath of life eternal,
rejoice in his renown.

                Ruined are the days,
gone glorious rewards   the rich of earth gave out.
Now neither kings   nor noble emperors
95   nor gold-dispensing lords   in glory live,
accustomed lordly fame,   as formerly:
deeply fallen this nobility,   departed its delights.
The worst of men remain   and rule the world
they labor in: brought low is glory thus.
100 Great men of earth   grow old and wither,
all men wither now   the world throughout;
old-age takes one   with ashen face:
grey-head grieving   finds his friend
from royal birth   returned to earth.
105 Not then can flesh-home,   failing life,
sweetness suck   or sorrow know,
hand arouse   or heart desire.
Though brother with gold   his brother's grave adorn,
and bury him   with bright gifts
110 beside the dead,   do not believe
earth's treasures   truly time outlast.
Not for soul   sick with sins
in fear of God   can gold be consolation:
miser meets but misery,   unmitigated death.
115

Great is the awe of God: the earth before Him turns.
He lays foundations,   firm ground,
expanse of earth,   eternal heavens too.

Dull is he who does not dread the Lord:
120   death comes to him
unseen.
Blessed he who humbly lives:
                                    Heaven mercy heralds him
with faith, true confidence in God:
125   Creator spirit-strengthens him.

TRANSLATION NOTES

My translation of *The Seafarer* arises from a reading of the poem as religious, ecstatic, and unified. I take note of the critically-belabored problems of transition between text-lines 33a–33b and between 64a–64b, and yet I finally see the driving ecstasy of the poet conquering, justifying, making sense of, even requiring, these leaps. I do claim for myself the liberty of shearing the poem's tail (text-lines 109–124) which, besides being somewhat muddled syntactically, is more homiletic afterthought than poetic elaboration, and remains, at the least, a liability. Therefore, I follow Sweet in closing with the beautiful hypermetric lines advising us what to be on the lookout for!

The poet is not a sailor. He is not an old man muttering at the mercy of his memory. He is not advising a young deckhand. By imaginative transmigration, in a ship of ecstasy whose oars are wings, he embarks on a journey home, beyond the cycle of seasons and of fortune, to the keeping of God. He tells us in 58 and following that in his journey his "spirit" (llyge) is his guide. He but follows his spirit, which flies on ahead to chart the way. And then in 70: "I contemplate that way". The poem is that contemplation.

There are no "traditional" themes here. Nothing conceived in ecstasy is traditional. The transition which occurs after text line 33a is indeed a transition, but not a thematic one. I prefer to think of it, and to render it in my translation, as a modulation, a shift in key, a rhythmic intensification.

The sea-journey is a rite of passage. In preparation for his spiritual communion with God, the poet has exiled himself from men, from the earth, and from the cycle of life which dwelling on the earth implies: the growth and decay of natural things, the rise and fall of men and of the dwellings with which men adorn the land. The sea, with all the real dangers of passage on the sea, signifies, or rather discloses, makes comprehensible and thus real for the poet (and, incidentally, for the reader) the place of exile and the emotional and intellectual dimensions of that place of exile into which the poet as pilgrim has willed himself, his new residence. The poet calls forth from within himself the "true words" which will reveal where in his willed exile he has been led, and what he has suffered there, and why. The metaphor of the sea-journey is entirely appropriate. At 33b, the poet does not contemplate suicide, but rather in the ecstasy of his imagination longs for the consummation of communion. He says, "thoughts drive me out: what's death to me!" And the translation at 41 reads: "a pilgrim's calling, pursue a pilgrim's home," a line which I have chosen willfully to echo at 56 because the goal and the direction of the poet's thought opens out so clearly before us in this line. The transition at text-line 64b is also a modulation. At 33b, the poet's thoughts "beat boldly;" at 64b, having turned back completely upon himself in self-imposed, spiritual exile, these thoughts strike fire, and the poem speaks of the "fire of the ecstasy of dwelling close to God." What follows in the poem is a true contemplation: a meditation on the cyclical nature of life and at the sadness and deception attendant upon a full commitment to that which must fall, die, disappear.

Translation Line No.

1   "awake and sing": beside being justified by the closeness of *wrecan* and *wreccan*, articulates the ecstatic origin of the poem: that which has been asleep becomes awakened. The "true words" are not merely a communication of the experience of the poet, but are actually the wings upon which the poet rides in his ecstasy.

7-8   Prose order would require: "through darkest nights the dark cliffs loomed above the plunging ship." Note here and elsewhere that I have tried to preserve an alliterative structure; however, at times (not here) I have tricked the strict tradition by alliterating the second stress of the second half-line. Where I have done so, I have felt the violation of the old poetics justified by the generation of better sound patterns within the translated line. Also note that I have let pass by, in the pleasure of euphony, occasional equivalent vowel alliterations within whole lines. I have worked to preserve the stress pattern, but here, as elsewhere, ecstasy cannot be held accountable for an occasional slip of the tongue.

15   "paths of exile, exile-vows I held." An attempt to render the poet's double intention in th e use of "last": (1) masculine = path, track; (2) neuter = vow, obligation. The words are alike in form in the dative plural. Of course, the poet as pilgrim would see his dedication to God, his willed exile from the life of men, as a vow.

19–22   An improvement. Malone and Raffel are inadequate here.

29–30   "Death-risks/ and adversaries few" amplifies "bealosiþa hwōn".

31–32   "cannot comprehend that I continue/must abide my exile on the sea" supplies the poet's implication that his exile is willed. "must" is appropriate because of the vow ("last") into which he has entered.

35   "cold harvest that!" for "corna caldast".

38   "thoughts drive me out: what's death to me?" It is quite literally, as the poet says, his thoughts which impel him forward, until the moment when the spirit flies forth from his body, not in death, but in true communion. "What' s death to me?" is the rhetorical quest ion which follows logically, and at the same time opens cataclysmically, the full dimension of the poet's thought at this point, the deep abyss at the ledge of which he stands, about to let go his connection with firm ground. Of course, that flight to communion does not occur in the poem itself, which remains, despite its ecstatic origins and traditional modulations, earth-bound, as must all creations of *homo faber*.

43   "Dryhten": the Christian Lord

51   "longunge", besides "longing", includes in its force-field "weariness", "sadness", "dejection"

53   "dwellings adorn the land": reading *byrig*, nominative plural, as "dwellings", and giving to the half-line (48b in the text) the sense which I think the poet intended: man's dwellings on earth, like all things which arise from the earth, from the land, are ephemeral.

54   "Death-cycles": the translator's interpretation of the poet's vague "ealle þa" (text-line 50).

58b   "soon fruit ripened falls" is the conclusion to be drawn from the sadness and sorrow which summer's guardian calls forth in the poet. Fruit is to be understood as all that which is produced by the earth.

59–61   An amplification of line 55a in the text.

62   "self-satisfied": an attempt at rendering the force behind the compound "seft-eadig" which, literally, would be "soft-happy". "Prosperous", or "blissful" and "lucky", as Malone would have it, will not do. The gelatinous quality attributed to the character of the man upon whom the epithet "seft-eadig" is fixed must not, at the same time, be allowed to absorb all of the scorn which the poet levels upon such a one who has not "ventured". The result is the withering condemnation "self-satisfied".

63   An indulging alliterative pleasure.

64   The crux of the translation. Strictly, an ecstasy, a displacement: the spirit places itself, or is placed, outside the body as it nears communion. I do not follow closely the correlative structure of the text, which explains the "for-þon" ("for that reason") of text-line 58 by the "forþon" ("because") of 64. In the translation, the sheer ecstasy of the homing spirit actually moves the spirit to words (!), that is, a one and one-half line speech.

70b–72a An amplification of text-lines 64b–65a. "Hatran" = hot, inspiring, flaming. The modulation and intensification cannot be overlooked at this point. The poet moves into high gear.

75b–76a A rendering of "ær his tīdege to twēon weorþeð" (text 69).

85   "all false gods": the implication of a pagan and Christian blend in "deōfle".

90   "gone glorious rewards": "onmēdlan," beyond its meanings s of pomp and glory, has also the sense of "that which consists of rewards or wages." The meaning of the passage (text lines 80b-90b) is not merely that at one time in the past life on earth was more splendid and therefore more desirable than contemporary life, but rather that even the admittedly glorious kings and emperors of yesterday (note the conscious linguistic reference to a Caesar), those who more than anyone, could have been expected to construct firm foundations and boundaries, have perished, have disappeared. The implication is that only now, in the time of the poet, when "all men wither now the world throughout" (text-line 90), has God chosen to reveal the true ephemeral nature of the world, of that which is created, an emphemerality which the glory of the past, in its glittering diversions, may have concealed.

100   Another curio from the curiosity shop of free alliteration patterns.

111   "miser meets but misery   unmitigated death": To appreciate the concision here, one need only read the abortive attempt of Malone to release this concept in his lines 100–103.

112b   "the earth before Him turns": The text is: "for-þon hī sēo molde oncyrreð". If this is the meaning of text 103b, we can only bow before the conceptual (and spatial or geometrical) depth and profundity of the poet's mind.

113   We note in the text the number of times, at the close, the idea of God's establishing "firm foundations" appears: "gesta elade" in 104a, "gestaþelað" in 108a, "staþelum" in the discarded tail.

116   "spirit-strengthens": a rendering of "makes firm" (gestaþelað) "the spirit for him."

INDEX OF FIRST LINES

A calculation of attitudes—..71

A cotton dress, up and over..9

A drawing of rainbow fish..10

A white-haired woman 30

Against my naked chest 32

Always as the stone is placed 137

An empty road, the sun is out..104

And flowers then in spring..145

And I will come to know this long sleep 147

And if it were because of her—..103

And into April birds lift sheer blue sky..144

And so, suddenly one dies 113

And this the sea— 102

And winter: that year the ice 139

And words words explanations 153

Ares Gold-Changer of bodies 180

As I am in the room 132

Attendant upon the wild woman..82

Back to the beginning 25

Before, during, and after..68

Beyond death—recovery 60

But refuge…?..96

But to speak out— 99

Come into my house 28

Control of the pancreas, liver, spleen..95

Did he master all the necessary moments..160

Divine is the archer's body 23

Flocks of light-dreaming birds.. 195

Granted the irreplaceable pleasures 57

Happy, happy the thronging of the butterflies.......................... 162

He had come closer 51

Heavy is the People's talk 182

Hope and honour-bound 107

How painful then to see the vanity 152

How was it that we came 108

I bought you schedules, saw you off... 118

I had to erase my life 15

I have not seen you for so long 37

I have spent the day alone 112

I have taken all the rocks you love 4

I send you flowers potted 128

I walked out late to visit you 140

I was led to consider the rocky coast 39

I was with Socrates in the court at Athens 166

I watch him from a distance.. 121

I would not say—... 61

In alliance held... 94

In deep woods through autumn 154

In Dreams appear the Visions.. 178

In the country 63

In the darkness I am a free-fall diver 165

In the grotto against the mountain 6

In the morning, intersecting echoes 98

In the room at the end of the corridor...................................... 14

In the wind, of these.. 88

In the woods, only a few insects buzzing 22

It is, yes, that one sees 65

It was over, the encompassing fatigue..77

It was to be the last exhibition 74

It was what I wanted...58

Lady you are inside my heart 150

Later, much later...44

Life zones of lepidoptera..109

Loud-ringing the stroke of Zeus..172

Mist here—in the valleys...114

My lungs were burning in a dream 100

No one among those 84

Not to yield...64

Not you but places strange cities 149

Nothing in the paper once again 122

Now grass I see and ferns 117

Nowhere is the limit...70

Numbers, and where have you slipped away 33

O moth, you blow through the air 38

O violet flower...21

On the edge (ledge) 90

On the riverbank 31

On this hill...35

Once gone She left behind..176

Open! the key, the lock, the gate...45

Or, conduct a truce...97

Personified preconditions of flight...83

Portrait: you at midnight...138

Rows of vertical mirrors 17

She rages in her room 123

Silence mathematically conceived 93

Silent for so long...52

Sing the dream songs 69

So be it—nothing from this moment 89

So if you please to be 115

So on to other things 148

Someone on the fringe 91

Still water dark ground 111

Still, I have my books 125

Subtle wise resourceful in his Skill 198

Symbolic wounds 73

The birds have not come 142

The church music, an organ 16

The day I took you to the hospital 126

The Etruscan singer fingers the strings 34

The flowers drove their stems 18

The horse-loving lord 188

The lanterns in the dark forest 47

The message that I send 141

The mystery of heights 49

The needle of the compass twirls 12

The one and only way 66

The opera singer who lives across the street 161

The projection of precedence 59

The proposition was not to discover 75

The sand undulates across the dunes 26

The shadow of the rose-bush 8

The shadows of the trees 29

The taste of things to come 163

The tendency to cogitate 56

The touch—to render 76

The wind blows outside 129

There are herds of horses 20

There is no use in waiting 143

There was horizon's level plain 167

There was no sky tonight— 101

There. Here. Now. What? 78

This land of echoes 164

Thoroughgoing uncertainty— 67

Through the unmown grass 24

Till then, nothing was known 86

To achieve (unmarred) 46

To be convinced 53

To be deprived of living 43

To be disillusioned 62

To be useless 55

To capture the rapture of— 92

To have become (alone) 81

To speak to you my language 151

To this day, this and no other 158

To visit Venice as a child 50

True words from myself may I awake and sing 200

Turn, and turn again 157

Under the hill I can hear 7

We cycled then through half of Europe 124

What art is this? 5

What grotesque dance 27

When dark the water in the pond 110

Where did Goya store the bloody limbs 36

Where? How? When? 11

While I sit in my shade 13

Whispering, going to the sacrifice 72

Who weilds with reverence 186
Who will ever understand you 3
Winter light— 87
Wittgenstein: doubt 54
Yes, you see the view 48
You of all people 85
You turn over into my hands 19
You vow to die. Tonight 127
You will think I have for other reasons 116
Your last night you cooked the dinner 146
ΑΡΙΣΤΟΝ ΜΕΝ ΗΥΔΟΡ Water is best 184
ΔΑΜΕΝΤΑ ΦΡΕΝΑΣ ΙΜΕΡΩΙ Poseidon 192
ΚΑΙ ΦΘΕΓΜΑ ΚΑΙ ΑΝΕΜΟΕΝ 196
ΠΕΙΘΩ She Persuasion 174
ΠΟΛΛΑ ΤΑ ΔΕΙΝΑ Many the strange things 193
ΧΑΡΙΣ transforms all things 190
Ω ΖΕΥ ΒΑΣΙΛΕΥ Zeus King 170